100 fac

SOLAR SYSTEM

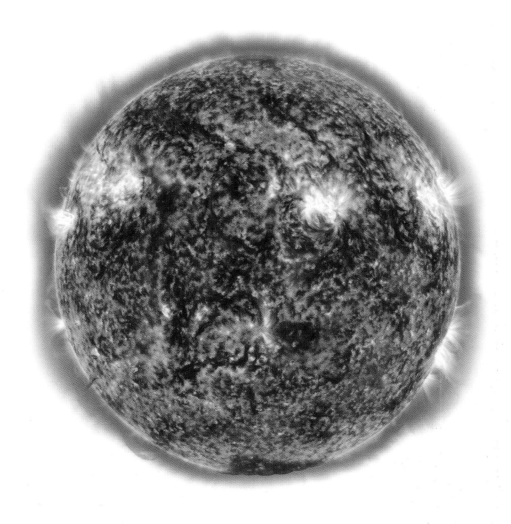

100 facts

SOLAR SYSTEM

Ian Graham

Consultant: Sue Becklake

Miles Kelly

First published in 2015 by Miles Kelly Publishing Ltd
Harding's Barn, Bardfield End Green, Thaxted, Essex, CM6 3PX, UK

2 4 6 8 10 9 7 5 3 1

PUBLISHING DIRECTOR Belinda Gallagher
CREATIVE DIRECTOR Jo Cowan
EDITORIAL DIRECTOR Rosie Neave
EDITOR Amy Johnson
DESIGNERS Andrea Slane, Joe Jones
IMAGE MANAGER Liberty Newton
INDEXER Jane Parker
PRODUCTION Elizabeth Collins, Caroline Kelly
REPROGRAPHICS Stephan Davis, Jennifer Cozens, Thom Allaway

ISBN 978-1-78209-646-7

Printed in China

British Library Cataloguing-in-Publication Data
A catalogue record for this book is available from the British Library

ACKNOWLEDGEMENTS
The publishers would like to thank the following artists who have contributed to this book:
Stuart Jackson-Carter, Mike Foster (Maltings Partnership)
All other artwork from the Miles Kelly Artwork Bank

The publishers would like to thank the following sources for the use of their photographs:
Key: t = top, b = bottom, l = left, r = right, c = centre, m= main, bg = background, ut = used throughout
Cover: (front) Jurgen Ziewe/Alamy, (back, t) Muskoka Stock Photos/Shutterstock.com
Alamy 10(m) NG Images; 30(tr) Galaxy Picture Library **Corbis** 22(b) YONHAP/epa; 27(tr) Caren Brinkema/Science Faction;
34(b) NASA – JPL, (cr) NASA; 41(tr) **European Space Agency (ESA)** 13(br) ESA-Anneke Le Floc'h; 25(bl) ESA/ÖWF/P. Santek;
35(br) NASA/JPL/Space Science Institute **Glow Images** 24(t) SuperStock, (cr) Stocktrek Images/Walter Myers; 31(m) Stocktrek
Images/Ron Miller; 36(m) Sciepro/Science Photo Library **NASA** 2–3; 5(b) NASA Jet Propulsion Laboratory (NASA/JPL);
8(b) MPIA/NASA/Calar Alto Observatory, (t) NASA, C.R.O; 13(cl), (bl); 17(b); 24(c) NASA/JPL; 25(timeline, tl) NASA/JPL-
Caltech, (timeline, tr) NASA/JPL-Caltech, (timeline, bl) NASA/JPL-Caltech/MSSS, (timeline, br) NASA/JPL-Caltech/MSSS;
26(br) NASA/JPL; 27(bl) NASA/JPL/JHUAPL; 30(bl); 33(tr) NASA/JPL-Caltech/SSI; 35(bl) ESA/NASA/JPL/University of Arizona,
(c) NASA/JPL/Space Science Institute, (cr) Cassini Imaging Team, SSI, JPL, ESA, NASA; 36(br) NASA/JPL; 37(bl) NASA/JPL/
USGS, (bc), (br); 38(br) Voyager 2, NASA; 39(t) Voyager Project, JPL, NASA, (br) Voyager 2, NASA; 44(bl) GReat Images in
NASA (NASA-GRIN), (br) NASA/JPL-Caltech/Malin Space Science Systems; 47(tl) Debra Meloy Elmegreen (Vassar College) et al.,
& the Hubble Heritage Team (AURA/STScI/NASA), (bl) NASA, ESA, K. Noll (STScI) **Photoshot** 20(r) **Rex Features** 45(cr) REX/
Everett Collection **Science Photo Library** 9(m) David A. Hardy; 11(r) Claus Lunau; 15(b) Royal Astronomical Society; 18(b) Mark
Garlick; 19(tr); 22(cr) Ria Novosti; 26(tl) Mark Garlick; 32(b) Mark Garlick; 37(t) Mark Garlick; 41(bl) ESA/Rosetta/Philae/
ROLIS/DLR; 45(tl) NASA; 47(cr) Detlev van Ravenswaay **Shutterstock.com** 1 Triff; 5(tc) MarcelClemens; 6(t, bg) fluidworkshop,
(cl, ut) STILLFX; 6–7(labels, ut) clickthis; 7(cr) A Aleksii; 9(quiz panel, ut) caesart, (cr, bl, br) Picsfive; 10(b) studio online, (tr) Dimec,
(IDBI panel, ut) fluidworkshop; 11(br) studio online, (bl) Alan Uster; 12(graph paper, ut) Stephen Rees; 13(b, bg) nuttakit,
(cl, bl, br) Picsfive; 14(br) Terrance Emerson; 15(cr) Natursports, (b, bg) Filipchuk Oleg; 16(tr); 17(tl) Redsapphire, (tr) Snowbelle,
(t, bg) nuttakit; 18–19(t) Rafael Pacheco; 19(bc) Stephen Aaron Rees; 20–21(bg) zhuda; 20(activity panel, ut) Shawn Hine,
(c) Dimec; 21(diagram, Moon) Rafael Pacheco, (diagram, Sun) Triff, (br) Thomas Nord; 22(tr) Muskoka Stock Photos,
(tr, cr) Fenton one; 23(panel, tr) MarcelClemens, (panel, bl) ChinellatoPhoto, (panel, br) ChinellatoPhoto, (bl) Galyna Andrushko;
27(b, bg) nuttakit; 28–29(labels) Aleksandr Bryliaev; 31(tl, bg) studio online; 42(t, bg) evv; 44–45(book bg) Valentin Agapov,
44–45(screen bg) fluidworkshop; 47(frames) fluidworkshop **Superstock** 6–7(bg) imageBROKER; 14(tl) Science and Society;
15(t) Stocktrek Images; 20(bl) Miloslav Druckmuller; 31(br) and 36(bl) Science and Society

Every effort has been made to acknowledge the source and copyright holder of each picture.
Miles Kelly Publishing apologizes for any unintentional errors or omissions.

Made with paper from a sustainable forest

www.mileskelly.net   info@mileskelly.net

The publishers would like to thank the Society for Popular
Astronomy for their help in compiling this book.

CONTENTS

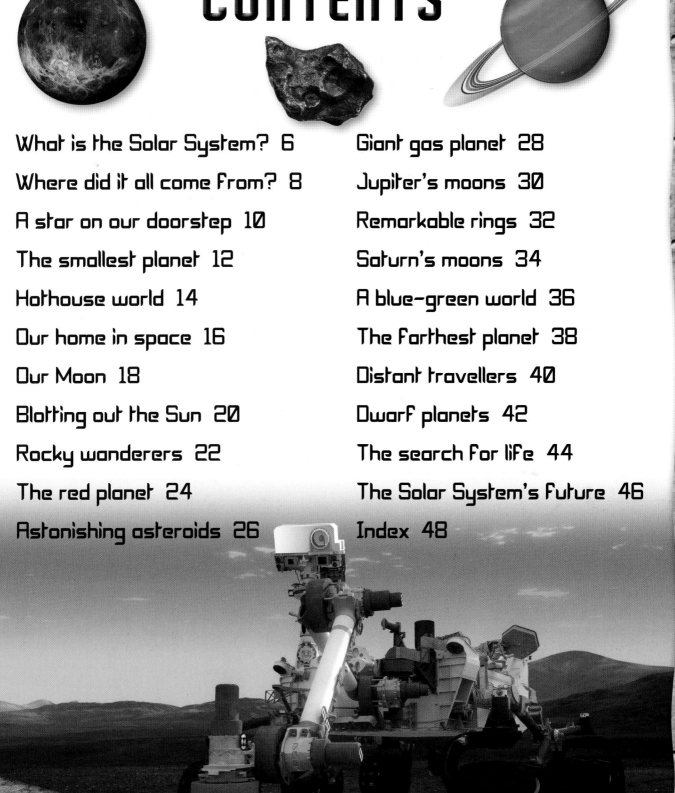

What is the Solar System?

1 The Solar System consists of the Sun and everything that orbits (moves around) it. Eight planets orbit the Sun, and more than 160 smaller moons orbit the planets. There are also millions of other objects circling the Sun, including asteroids and comets. The pull of the Sun's gravity holds the Solar System together.

EARTH

URANUS

SATURN

NEPTUNE

MARS

◄ The four planets closest to the Sun — Mercury, Earth, Venus and Mars — are smaller and made of rock. The four farthest from the Sun — Jupiter, Saturn, Uranus and Neptune — are bigger and made of gas and liquid.

JUPITER

Where did it all come from?

2 The Solar System began as a vast, swirling cloud of gas and dust called a nebula. Most of it was made of hydrogen, the lightest and most common element in the Universe.

3 Around 4.6 billion years ago, the Solar System began to form. It may have been started by the huge explosion of a star – a supernova. Shock waves from the giant explosion would have compressed (squashed) the nebula. Gravity then took over, pulling the nebula inwards and causing it to collapse in on itself.

▼ An area of the Orion nebula in which new stars are forming. Billions of years ago, a nebula like this contained everything needed for the Solar System to form.

▼ This photograph of the remains of a star that exploded in 1572 has been coloured to show what's happening inside it.

Gas and particles (green and yellow) are flying out in all directions

The outside edge of the explosion, called a shock wave, is shown in blue

Hot dust (red) was made when the star exploded

4 As the nebula collapsed inwards, it started spinning. Clumps of gas and dust formed in the collapsing cloud and grew bigger as gravity pulled more and more gas and dust towards them. A dense mass formed at the centre of the nebula, which increased in temperature and eventually became our Sun. The remaining gas and dust flattened into a spinning disc, later forming the planets.

5 There are still signs of the spinning motion of the shrinking nebula today. The Sun, planets and moons all spin, and the planets travel around the Sun.

▼ It took about 100 million years for the planets to form from the nebula.

1. Dust particles and tiny bits of rock in the spinning disc clumped together.

3. The balls of rock and gas grew bigger and bigger, eventually forming the planets.

2. As these clumps grew bigger their gravity pulled more dust and rock towards them.

A star on our doorstep

WARNING!
NEVER look directly at the Sun! It is so bright that it can damage your eyes and even cause blindness.

6 The Sun is the star at the centre of our Solar System. It looks so much bigger than the other stars in the sky because it's much closer to us. It's about 150 million kilometres from Earth.

▶ Earth (right) is a tiny speck compared to a vast tongue of glowing gas erupting from the Sun (above).

7 The Sun looks small in the sky, but it's a giant compared to Earth. It's so huge that 109 Earths would fit side by side across its middle.

I DON'T BELIEVE IT!
Before scientists worked out what really makes the Sun shine, they thought it might be a giant lump of coal burning in space!

8 The Sun is made of super-hot gases — mostly hydrogen and helium. Its core (centre) is the hottest part. The temperature here is as high as 15 million°C.

▶ Gravity tries to make the Sun smaller while heat from the core tries to make it bigger. The two are in balance.

10 About four million tonnes of the Sun's mass vanishes every second! This happens because nuclear fusion changes some of the Sun's mass into energy. The Sun has been losing this huge amount of mass every second for about 4.6 billion years.

9 Scientists worked out how the Sun shines in the 1920s. The extremely high pressure in the Sun's core causes particles of hydrogen to smash into each other and fuse (stick together) to form a new substance, helium. This is called nuclear fusion. Every time it happens, energy is given out.

Corona
The outer part of the Sun's atmosphere

Chromosphere
The lowest layer of the Sun's atmosphere

Photosphere
The visible surface of the Sun

Core
Nuclear reactions give out energy

Convective zone
Hot gas rises towards the surface, and falls back inside the Sun in currents

Radiative zone
Energy radiates out from the core

▼ Light and warmth from the Sun sustain life on Earth.

11 Energy produced by nuclear fusion travels from the Sun's core to its surface. This takes up to 200,000 years. Then when it leaves the Sun, it takes just over eight minutes to reach Earth.

12 Mercury is the Sun's closest planet. It's also the smallest in the Solar System – a tiny planet less than half the size of Earth. It is made of rock with a big iron core, and is very dense for its size.

13 Planets closer to the Sun have to travel through space faster than those farther away, or they would be pulled into the Sun. Mercury's orbit takes 88 Earth days. However, it spins so slowly that a day on Mercury lasts 176 Earth days.

▼ Mercury is a small world that looks similar to Earth's Moon.

14 Mercury has one of the biggest impact craters in the Solar System. It's called the Caloris Basin and it measures 1550 kilometres across. It was caused when an object about 100 kilometres across smashed into Mercury.

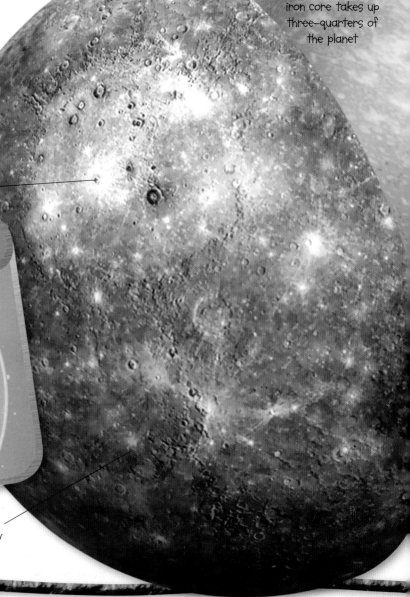

Mercury's huge iron core takes up three-quarters of the planet

The Caloris Basin is a vast shallow crater, surrounded by mountains 2 kilometres high

Fact file: MERCURY

Named after: The messenger of the Roman gods
Diameter: 4879 kilometres (0.38 times Earth)
Distance from the Sun: 58 million kilometres
Time to spin once: 59 days
Time to orbit the Sun: 88 days
Average temperature: 167°C
Number of moons: 0

The surface of Mercury is scarred by thousands of craters

15 The side of Mercury that faces the Sun reaches up to 430°C. That's hot enough to melt tin! The temperature on the side facing away from the Sun drops to –180°C. That's the biggest difference in temperature between the two sides of any planet in the Solar System.

A thin crust of rock floats on top of the mantle

A layer of rock, called the mantle, surrounds the core

QUIZ

1. How long does it take Mercury to orbit the Sun?
2. What is Mercury's large core made of?
3. Which spacecraft was the first to visit Mercury?

Answers:
1. 88 Earth days 2. Iron 3. Mariner 10

16 Only two spacecraft have visited Mercury so far. Mariner 10 was the first in the 1970s. A second spacecraft called Messenger arrived in 2008. A third spacecraft, BepiColombo, is due to launch in 2016.

◀ Mariner 10 took the first close-up photographs of Mercury as it flew past in 1974.

▲ Messenger was the first spacecraft to go into orbit around Mercury, in 2011.

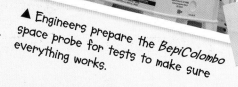

▲ Engineers prepare the BepiColombo space probe for tests to make sure everything works.

13

Hothouse world

▲ Venus is surrounded by a thick blanket of sulphuric acid clouds.

17 **The second planet from the Sun, Venus, is about the same size as Earth.** It is also the closest planet to Earth, although the two are very different. Its rocky surface is hidden under a very thick carbon dioxide atmosphere that traps the Sun's heat, making it the Solar System's hottest planet.

▶ Venus is one of the brightest objects in the sky, because its thick clouds reflect a lot of sunlight.

Venus

18 **Venus spins more slowly than other Solar System planets.** It takes 243 Earth days to spin around once, compared to just 24 hours for Earth. Venus spins in the opposite direction to the other planets – the Sun rises in the east on Earth, but in the west on Venus.

I DON'T BELIEVE IT!

Venus's atmosphere is so dense that it has about 90 times the pressure of Earth's. You would need a spacecraft as strong as a submarine to land on Venus.

19 **One way to see Venus's surface is to use radar.** Radar can send radio waves from a spacecraft, through a planet's atmosphere to bounce off the surface below. Analyzing these reflections reveals the shape of the surface.

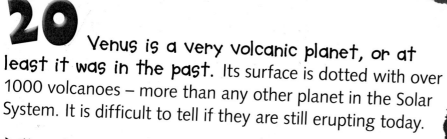

20 Venus is a very volcanic planet, or at least it was in the past. Its surface is dotted with over 1000 volcanoes – more than any other planet in the Solar System. It is difficult to tell if they are still erupting today.

▶ The surface of Venus is smooth in places, but it also has mountains, volcanoes, craters and canyons.

Fact file: VENUS

Named after: The Roman goddess of love and beauty
Diameter: 12,104 kilometres (0.95 times Earth)
Distance from the Sun: 108 million kilometres
Time to spin once: 243 days
Time to orbit the Sun: 225 days
Average temperature: 464°C
Number of moons: 0

▶ Watching Venus (the big black dot) crossing the Sun gave scientists enough information to work out the size of the Solar System.

21 The famous explorer Captain James Cook sailed from England to Tahiti to see Venus crossing between Earth and the Sun in 1769. The crossing was important to astronomers because they could use it to work out the size of the Solar System. By observing the time it took for Venus' shadow to cross the Sun, astronomers were able to calculate the distance between Earth and Venus.

▶ Captain James Cook and Charles Green, the astronomer on the expedition, both made drawings of Venus crossing the Sun.

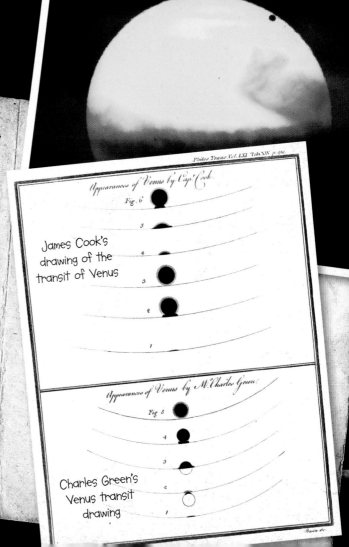

James Cook's drawing of the transit of Venus

Charles Green's Venus transit drawing

Our home in space

22 **Earth is the third planet from the Sun.** It is the only place in the Universe known to have liquid water and the ability to support life. It takes 24 hours to spin once, giving us night and day, and 365 days (a year) to orbit the Sun.

23 **One of the rocky planets, Earth consists of several layers.** The thin crust of rock that forms its surface sits on top of a deeper layer of rock called the mantle. Below the mantle, in the middle of the planet, there is a solid iron core with liquid iron around it.

▶ Life on Earth began in the oceans about 3.8 billion years ago and then spread across the whole planet.

24 **Earth's atmosphere is a mixture of gases, mainly nitrogen and oxygen.** It also contains some water vapour, carbon dioxide and tiny traces of other gases. This mixture of gases is called air, and without it life on Earth would not be possible.

◀ Earth's core is as hot as the surface of the Sun.

Crust

Upper mantle

Lower mantle

Liquid outer core

Solid inner core

5500°C   5000°C   4000°C   2000°C

I DON'T BELIEVE IT!
A day on Earth is 24 hours long today, but billions of years ago Earth was spinning much faster. A day was only 14 hours long. Earth's spin has been slowing down ever since.

▼ The weather changes from one season to the next because of Earth's tilt.

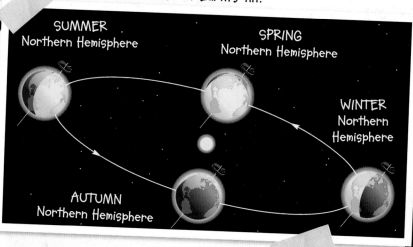

SUMMER
Northern Hemisphere

SPRING
Northern Hemisphere

WINTER
Northern Hemisphere

AUTUMN
Northern Hemisphere

▼ Earth's magnetic field extends far out into space. It protects us from the 'solar wind' – charged particles streaming out of the Sun.

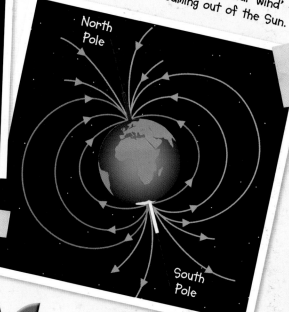

North Pole

South Pole

25 Earth tilts as it travels around the Sun, like a spinning top leaning over. This tilt produces the seasons. When the North Pole tilts towards the Sun, the northern half of Earth is warmer and the southern half is colder. As Earth moves around the Sun, the North Pole tilts away from the Sun. The northern half of Earth cools and the southern half warms up.

26 Earth behaves like a giant magnet with a north pole and a south pole. Liquid iron swirling around in Earth's core creates electrical currents that produce its magnetic field.

27 Particles flying out of the Sun cause an eerie glow in the sky called an aurora. Earth's magnetic field steers the particles into the upper atmosphere near the North and South poles. Here they collide with particles of gas, making them glow.

Fact file: EARTH

Named after: An old English word for the ground or soil
Diameter: 12,756 kilometres
Distance from the Sun: 149.6 million kilometres
Time to spin once: 23.9 hours
Time to orbit the Sun: 365.2 days
Average temperature: 15°C
Number of moons: 1

◄ Auroras light up the sky near the poles, seen from the International Space Station (left). They are known as the Northern Lights (*Aurora Borealis*) and Southern Lights (*Aurora Australis*).

Our Moon

28 Earth has one moon orbiting it.

The Moon is made of rock, and is about 384,000 kilometres from Earth. It is just over a quarter of the size of Earth. The Moon's surface is as dry as dust, and covered with thousands of craters made by rocks crashing into it from space.

▶ The big, dark patches on the Moon's surface were once thought to be seas. They are actually volcanic plains formed by lava flows that took place billions of years ago.

29 Scientists think the Moon was part of Earth until about 4.4 billion years ago.

Soon after Earth formed, a Mars-sized object crashed into it. The impact knocked chunks of rock out of Earth. The debris collected together, forming the Moon. Life never began on the Moon, as its gravity wasn't strong enough to hold onto an atmosphere.

▼ The Moon exists because of a cosmic collision billions of years ago.

3. The rock clumps together to form the Moon

1. A large wandering body collides with Earth

2. Rock from Earth as well as the destroyed body swirls around Earth

QUIZ

1. How old is the Moon?
2. Which space probe took the first photograph of the far side of the Moon?
3. Why is the pull of the Moon's gravity much weaker than Earth's?

Answers:
1. About 4.4 billion years 2. Luna 3 3. The Moon is much smaller than Earth

30 From Earth, we always see the same side of the Moon. This happens because the Moon spins at the same speed as it travels around Earth. The Moon's far side was seen for the first time when the Soviet *Luna 3* space probe photographed it in 1959. The first people to see the far side with their own eyes were the crew of the American *Apollo 8* mission in December 1968.

▲ The first image of the far side of the Moon. The far side has a thicker crust, and more craters than the side we see from Earth.

31 The tides that rise and fall on Earth are caused by the Moon. The Moon's gravity pulls Earth's oceans towards it. The water piles up in a big swollen bulge on one side of Earth, with another bulge on the opposite side. As Earth spins, these piles of water sweep around the planet, causing the high tides.

The Moon's pull of gravity

Earth

▶ The Moon's gravity creates two high tides every day.

Low tide

▲ When the high tide passes, the sea level falls.

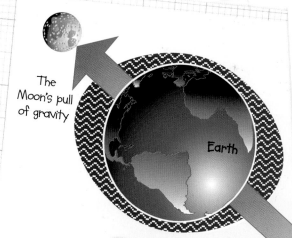

High tide

When the Sun, Moon and Earth are aligned, the added pull of the Sun's gravity creates extra-high tides

32 The Moon is much smaller than Earth, so its pull of gravity is weaker. Gravity gives you your weight, so you would weigh less on the Moon than on Earth. The Apollo astronauts who landed on the Moon weighed just one-sixth of their Earth weight while on the Moon.

Blotting out the Sun

33 The Moon sometimes passes between the Sun and Earth, casting a shadow on Earth. This is a solar eclipse. If it looks like the Moon is taking a bite out of the Sun, it's a partial eclipse. If the Moon covers the whole Sun, it's a total eclipse.

34 During a total solar eclipse, the Sun disappears behind the Moon, leaving just its bright corona (atmosphere) visible. It shows up as a glowing ring of light around the Moon. The Sun's atmosphere is incredibly hot – it reaches more than one million°C.

WARNING!
NEVER look directly at the Sun! It is so bright that it can damage your eyes and even cause blindness.

▲ These photographs, taken every four minutes, show a total solar eclipse from start to finish.

▼ The time during which the Moon completely hides the Sun is called totality.

FUTURE TOTAL ECLIPSES

DATE	VISIBLE FROM
9 March, 2016	Sumatra, Borneo, Sulawesi, Pacific Ocean
21 August, 2017	N Pacific Ocean, US, S Atlantic Ocean
2 July, 2019	S Pacific Ocean, Chile, Argentina
14 December, 2020	S Pacific Ocean, Argentina, Chile, S Atlantic Ocean

35

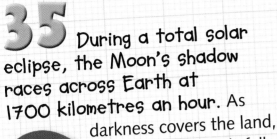

During a total solar eclipse, the Moon's shadow races across Earth at 1700 kilometres an hour. As darkness covers the land, birds and animals fall silent. They think night has come early!

36

How can the tiny Moon blot out the giant Sun? By a strange quirk of nature, the Moon is not only 400 times smaller than the Sun, it is also 400 times closer to Earth than the Sun. So, from Earth, the Sun and Moon look exactly the same size. This doesn't happen anywhere else in the Solar System.

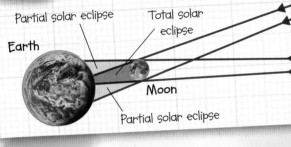

▼ During a total solar eclipse, the Moon blocks light rays from the Sun. People within the inner part of the Moon's shadow see a total eclipse. Those in the outer shadow see a partial eclipse.

Partial solar eclipse Total solar eclipse

Earth

Moon

Partial solar eclipse

Sun

37

The Sun, Earth and Moon can line up in a different way. If Earth comes between the Sun and Moon, it casts a shadow on the Moon. This is a lunar eclipse. Lunar eclipses can be partial or total. There are at least two lunar eclipses every year.

▶ A lunar eclipse occurs when the Moon moves through the Earth's shadow.

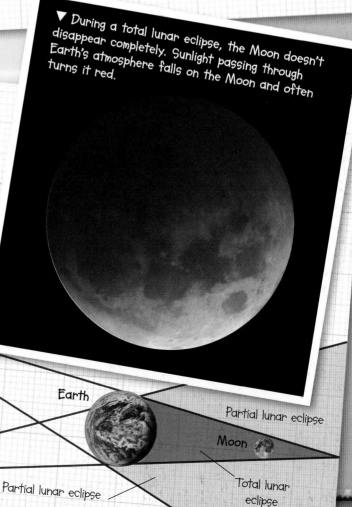

▼ During a total lunar eclipse, the Moon doesn't disappear completely. Sunlight passing through Earth's atmosphere falls on the Moon and often turns it red.

Sun

Earth

Moon

Partial lunar eclipse

Partial lunar eclipse

Total lunar eclipse

Rocky wanderers

38 If you see a streak of light in the sky, it's probably a meteor, or 'shooting star' (although they are not stars). Meteors are glowing streaks of light caused by pieces of space rock and dust burning up as they enter Earth's atmosphere.

39 Smaller space rocks burn up in the atmosphere, but bigger pieces can reach the ground. These cosmic arrivals are called meteorites. Most are small and land unseen, but sometimes a big one lands.

▲ Meteors streak across the sky in this picture of a meteor shower.

▲ This fireball was caught on camera over Chelyabinsk, Russia, on 15 February, 2013. It was caused by a space rock entering Earth's atmosphere from space and exploding over the city.

▶ Antarctica is a good place for meteorite-hunting, because the dark meteorites stand out from the white snow.

40
There are three main types of meteorites. They are stony (made of rock), iron (made of metal) and stony-iron (a mixture of rock and metal). Stony meteorites are the most common.

▲ Iron meteorites were once part of the core of a planet, moon or asteroid.

▲ Stony meteorites are made of minerals called silicates.

▲ Stony-iron meteorites contain equal amounts of metal and stone.

41
The biggest meteorite ever found in one piece weighs over 60 tonnes. It is a huge lump of metal known as the Hoba meteorite. It landed in Namibia, in Africa, around 80,000 years ago.

▼ The Hoba meteorite lay buried until a farmer discovered it in 1920 while ploughing his land. It remains in the same spot today.

FIND A METERORITE
You will need:
a magnet

Nearly all meteorites, even the stony ones, contain iron, so they can be picked up by a magnet. Look for dark, smooth, rounded rocks that are attracted to a magnet and feel heavy for their size.

42
Some meteorites come from the Moon or Mars. They were blasted out of the surface by other rocks smashing into them. They roamed the Solar System for millions of years before landing on Earth.

The red planet

43 Mars, the fourth planet from the Sun, is known as 'the red planet' due to its colour. It is the last of the terrestrial (Earth-like) planets, which are all made of rock and thought to have an iron core.

▼ The surface of Mars is a vast desert of fine red sand. It is dry, dusty and extremely cold, and has an atmosphere of poisonous carbon dioxide.

Fact file: MARS

Named after: The Roman god of war
Diameter: 6792 kilometres (0.53 times Earth)
Distance from the Sun: 228 million kilometres
Time to spin once: 24.6 hours
Time to orbit the Sun: 687 days
Average temperature: -65°C
Number of moons: 2

Olympus Mons

Valles Marineris

44 Mars has the biggest volcano in the Solar System, Olympus Mons. It's almost three times higher than Mount Everest. Mars also has one of the biggest canyons, Valles Marineris. It's nine times longer, 20 times wider and more than four times deeper than the Grand Canyon.

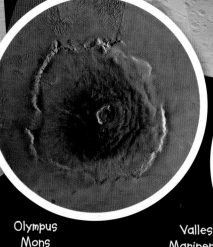

I DON'T BELIEVE IT!
In the 1890s astronomer Percival Lowell was convinced he could see canals on Mars, and that they must have been built by Martians. It was later proven that the canals didn't exist.

45 The north and south poles of Mars are covered with ice. They stay frozen all year round. During the Martian winter the poles get so cold that carbon dioxide from the atmosphere freezes onto them.

46 More than 20 spacecraft have been sent to Mars since the 1960s. They have flown past it, orbited it and landed on it. Four rovers have explored its surface. *Sojourner* was tiny, the size of a shoebox. *Spirit* and *Opportunity* were the size of golf buggys. *Curiosity* is the biggest yet, a nuclear-powered rover the size of a small car.

▼ The *Curiosity* rover was sent to Mars to explore its desert-like surface.

26 November, 2011: The rover is launched onboard an *Atlas 5* rocket. It is heading for a landing site in Gale Crater, 566 million kilometres away.

6 August, 2012: *Curiosity* is lowered onto the Martian surface by a rocket-powered Sky Crane. The landing is a success.

29 August, 2012: *Curiosity* begins its first drive to an area called Glenelg, about 400 metres from its landing site.

27 September, 2012: *Curiosity* returns images of what appears to be an ancient riverbed.

4 cm

10 October, 2012: *Curiosity* collects its first sample of Martian soil. The sample will be analyzed by its onboard instruments.

3 December, 2012: Through analzying soil, *Curiosity* discovers the first clear evidence that water once existed on Mars.

5 June, 2013: *Curiosity* prepares for its trip to the base of Mount Sharp, a journey of about 8 kilometres over rough terrain.

► This spacesuit and vehicle are being tested for a future manned mission to Mars.

47 There are plans to send astronauts to Mars later this century. A spaceflight would take up to nine months. Astronauts would then have to stay on Mars for another 18 months before the planets are close enough again for the return journey to Earth.

Astonishing asteroids

▼ Hundreds of thousands of asteroids orbit the Sun beyond the four inner planets. They are remains of the Solar System's formation.

48 Asteroids are huge chunks of rock and metal circling the Sun. Most orbit in a band between Mars and Jupiter called the Asteroid Belt. The biggest, Ceres, is 950 kilometres across.

49 Asteroid means 'star-like', because from Earth, asteroids look like tiny points of light. Astronomers can tell the difference between stars and asteroids because asteroids cross the sky faster than stars and often in a different direction. As an asteroid spins, the amount of light it reflects varies. By measuring these changes in brightness, astronomers can tell that most asteroids spin every 6–13 hours.

50 Some asteroids have their own moons. When the *Galileo* spacecraft was travelling through the Asteroid Belt on its way to Jupiter in 1993, it spotted an asteroid, named Ida, with a tiny moon orbiting it. It was the first asteroid found with its own moon. More than 150 asteroids are now known to have moons.

Ida

▼ Ida's moon was named Dactyl. It orbits Ida once every 20 hours, travelling about as fast as you could throw a ball.

Dactyl

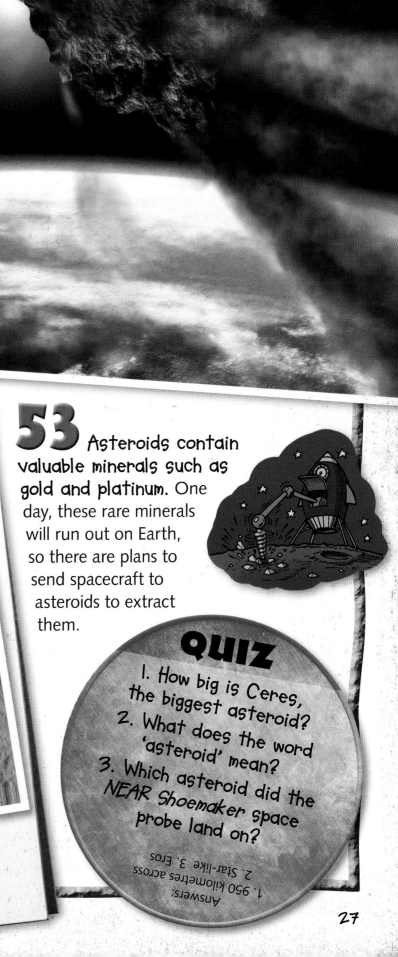

▶ The dinosaurs may have died out 66 million years ago when a large asteroid like this slammed into Earth.

51 Asteroids sometimes wander into our part of the Solar System. Asteroids that come close to Earth are called Near Earth Asteroids (NEAs). Over 10,000 NEAs have been discovered, but only a few hundred of them are big enough to be dangerous to Earth. Space is so vast that asteroids rarely hit Earth anyway. A large one hits Earth every 500,000 years or so.

52 In 1996, a space probe called NEAR Shoemaker was launched to study an asteroid called Eros. It orbited Eros for a year, collecting information, and then did something it wasn't designed to do – it landed on the asteroid. Controllers on Earth slowly lowered its orbit until it touched down. It's still there today.

▲ This is NEAR Shoemaker's last image of Eros. The bottom of the picture is blurred, because the signal was lost as the spacecraft touched down.

53 Asteroids contain valuable minerals such as gold and platinum. One day, these rare minerals will run out on Earth, so there are plans to send spacecraft to asteroids to extract them.

Giant gas planet

54 Jupiter is the Solar System's biggest planet. It is 11 times the size of Earth. Jupiter, along with Saturn, Uranus and Neptune, are known as gas giants, because they are huge planets made of gas and liquid.

55 Jupiter is made mainly of hydrogen and helium. Below its atmosphere, gas is compressed (squashed) so much that it changes to liquid. Deeper still it is compressed even more, causing the liquid to behave like metal. As Jupiter spins, this liquid metal creates a magnetic field, which is the strongest in the Solar System. At the centre there is thought to be a small, rocky core.

▶ Astronauts will never land on Jupiter, or any other gas giant, because there is no solid surface to touch down on.

Jupiter's thin atmosphere consists of layers of ammonia ice-clouds and water ice

Strong winds churn up many storms in Jupiter's atmosphere, like the Great Red Spot

Atmosphere

Hydrogen gas

Liquid hydrogen and helium

Metallic hydrogen and helium

Core

◀ Jupiter has a dense core about the size of Earth, surrounded by liquid and gas.

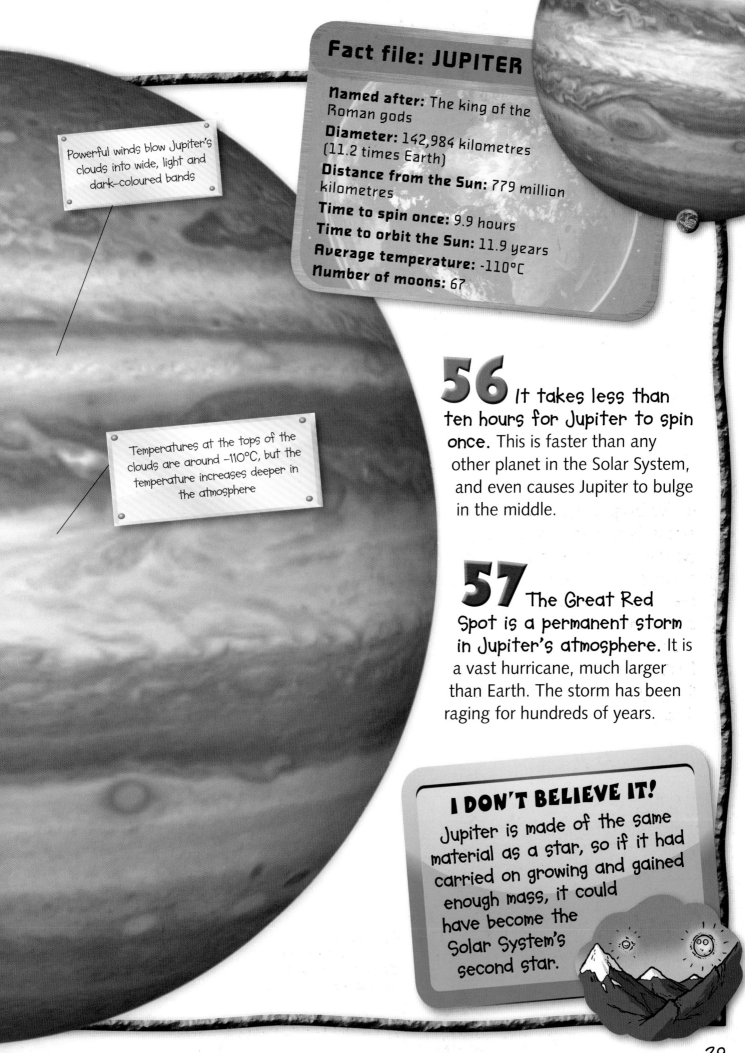

Powerful winds blow Jupiter's clouds into wide, light and dark-coloured bands

Fact file: JUPITER

Named after: The king of the Roman gods
Diameter: 142,984 kilometres (11.2 times Earth)
Distance from the Sun: 779 million kilometres
Time to spin once: 9.9 hours
Time to orbit the Sun: 11.9 years
Average temperature: -110°C
Number of moons: 67

Temperatures at the tops of the clouds are around -110°C, but the temperature increases deeper in the atmosphere

56 It takes less than ten hours for Jupiter to spin once. This is faster than any other planet in the Solar System, and even causes Jupiter to bulge in the middle.

57 The Great Red Spot is a permanent storm in Jupiter's atmosphere. It is a vast hurricane, much larger than Earth. The storm has been raging for hundreds of years.

I DON'T BELIEVE IT!

Jupiter is made of the same material as a star, so if it had carried on growing and gained enough mass, it could have become the Solar System's second star.

Jupiter's moons

58 Jupiter has more moons than any other planet. This is because of its huge size, as it means it has a very strong pull of gravity. So far, 67 moons have been discovered. The four biggest can be seen with binoculars. They're known as the Galilean moons, because they were seen for the first time by the Italian astronomer, Galileo Galilei, in 1610.

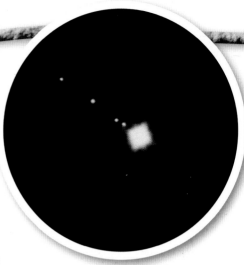

▲ Through a pair of binoculars, Jupiter's Galilean moons look like a line of stars alongside the planet.

59 The Galilean moons were a surprise for astronomers. These icy worlds all have very different features, and are not the dead, dusty worlds that scientists expected them to be.

▼ The Galilean moons were the first of Jupiter's moons to be discovered, and the first moons found orbiting another planet.

SPOTTING JUPITER

You will need:
a pair of binoculars

On a clear night, find the brightest 'star' in the sky. Look at it through your binoculars. If it has a line of tiny dots of light on one or both sides, you've found Jupiter – and its Galilean moons.

Io

Europa

Ganymede

Callisto

60 Jupiter's largest moon, Ganymede, is also the biggest in the Solar System. It is 1.5 times the size of our Moon. Ganymede is covered with a deep layer of ice. The second largest, Callisto, is the most heavily cratered object in the Solar System.

61 Io is the Solar System's most volcanically active moon. More than 150 volcanoes spew yellow, red and black sulphur onto its surface. One of its volcanoes, Loki, gives out more heat than all of Earth's active volcanoes combined.

▼ Volcanoes shoot plumes of sulphur up to 300 kilometres above Io.

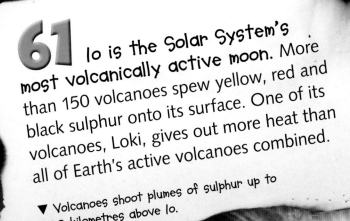

63 Four of Jupiter's smaller moons circle the gas giant within Io's orbit. They are called Metis, Adrastea, Amalthea and Thebe. All are odd shapes, as they don't have the mass needed to form a round, circular shape.

62 Europa is covered with unusually smooth ice. Scientists think the ice may be floating on an ocean of water, which is kept from freezing by the heat inside Europa. This ocean could be around 100 kilometres deep, and could contain life if conditions are right. In the future, probes may explore Europa's ocean for signs of life.

▲ Jupiter's moon Amalthea may be red because it is sprayed with sulphur from volcanoes on Io.

Remarkable rings

64 **Saturn is the Solar System's second biggest planet.** It is surrounded by huge, shining rings. Like Jupiter, Saturn is made almost completely of hydrogen and helium. Below its thin atmosphere, these gases are compressed so much that they become liquid.

Saturn gets its colour from sulphur in its atmosphere

The total width of Saturn's rings is about three-quarters of the distance from Earth to the Moon, but they are only a few hundred metres thick

▶ Saturn spins so fast that it bulges outwards at the middle.

65 **Millions of ice particles make up Saturn's rings.** This is what makes them so bright. They orbit the planet like tiny moons reflecting sunlight. The rings are thought to be the remains of destroyed moons, comets or asteroids.

The fierce winds blowing in Saturn's atmosphere form faint bands across its surface

◀ The ice in Saturn's rings ranges in size from specks smaller than a grain of sand to huge chunks.

66 Like the other gas giants, Saturn's upper atmosphere blows around the planet in bands. This means that gas is moved around at high speed, forming huge storms. Saturn is home to many storms, including vast hurricanes at its poles.

▲ The *Cassini* spacecraft spotted this hurricane at Saturn's North Pole in 2012, rotating at the centre of a huge, six-sided storm. This image has been coloured to show different cloud heights.

67 If you could find a big enough bath of water, Saturn would float in it. This is because despite its huge size, it has the lowest density of all the planets.

Gaps and bends in the rings are caused by the pull of gravity from nearby moons

I DON'T BELIEVE IT!
When Galileo first looked at Saturn through his telescope in 1610, he mistook the planet's rings for two moons.

Fact file: SATURN

Named after: The Roman god of agriculture
Diameter: 120,536 kilometres (9.5 times Earth)
Distance from the Sun: 1434 million kilometres
Time to spin once: 10.7 hours
Time to orbit the Sun: 29.4 years
Average temperature: -140°C
Number of moons: 62

Saturn's moons

68 **Saturn has nearly as many moons as Jupiter.** So far, 62 have been confirmed. Saturn and its moons were explored by the *Cassini* spacecraft, which arrived at Saturn in 2004. It discovered moons that are too small to be seen from Earth.

69 **Some of Saturn's moons orbit inside its rings.** These are called shepherd moons because they herd the ring particles together, like a shepherd keeping a flock of sheep together. Shepherd moons give Saturn's rings sharper edges.

▼ Saturn's shepherd moons, such as Atlas shown here, create the gaps in the planet's famous rings.

70 **Titan, Saturn's largest moon, is bigger than Mercury.** It is the only moon in the Solar System with a thick atmosphere. Since its arrival, *Cassini's* observations have allowed scientists to discover much more about the solid surface hidden below Titan's atmosphere.

▶ The *Cassini* spacecraft flew through a gap in Saturn's rings before going into orbit around the planet.

71 The European Space Agency landed a mini-probe called *Huygens* on Titan in 2005. It was carried to Saturn by the *Cassini* spacecraft. *Huygens* found lakes on Titan, but instead of water they're filled with chemicals including ethane and methane. *Huygens* also carried a microphone that picked up the sound of wind blowing on the moon. This was the first sound ever recorded on another planetary body.

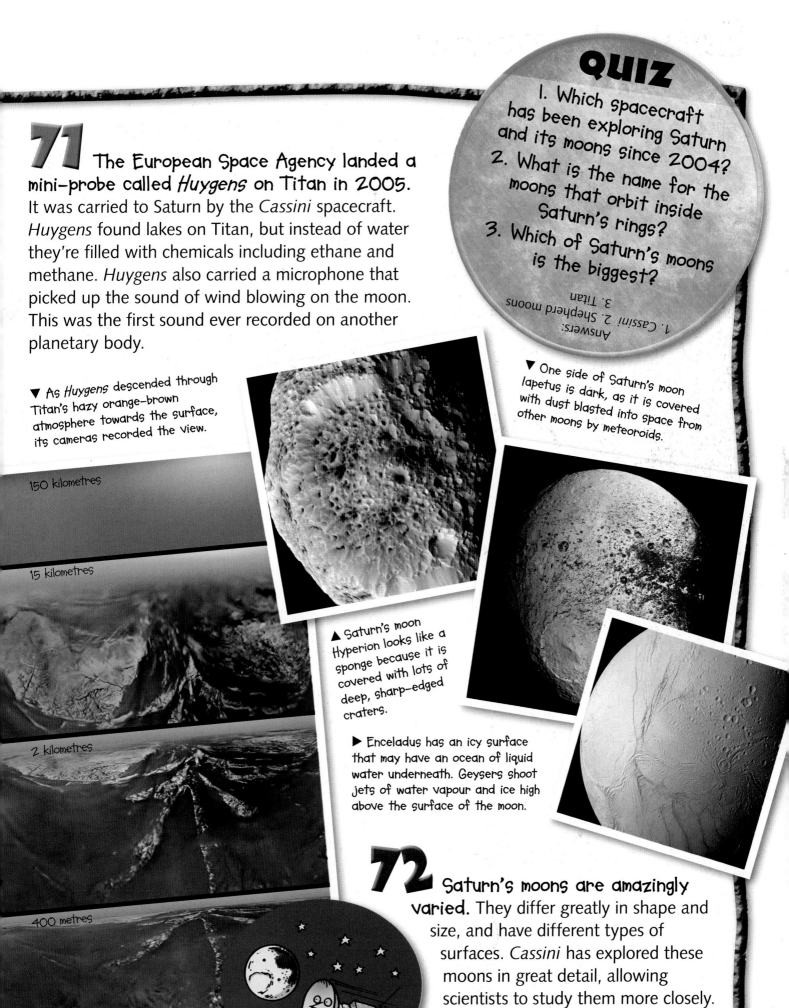

▼ As *Huygens* descended through Titan's hazy orange-brown atmosphere towards the surface, its cameras recorded the view.

150 kilometres

15 kilometres

2 kilometres

400 metres

▼ One side of Saturn's moon Iapetus is dark, as it is covered with dust blasted into space from other moons by meteoroids.

▲ Saturn's moon Hyperion looks like a sponge because it is covered with lots of deep, sharp-edged craters.

▶ Enceladus has an icy surface that may have an ocean of liquid water underneath. Geysers shoot jets of water vapour and ice high above the surface of the moon.

72 Saturn's moons are amazingly varied. They differ greatly in shape and size, and have different types of surfaces. *Cassini* has explored these moons in great detail, allowing scientists to study them more closely.

A blue-green world

73 Uranus, the seventh planet from the Sun, is about four times bigger than Earth. It has an atmosphere of hydrogen and helium. Below it is an ocean of liquid water, ammonia and methane surrounding a rocky core.

Dark, dusty rings

74 Unlike the other planets, Uranus spins on its side. This means that one pole faces the Sun for 42 years and then the other pole faces the Sun for 42 years. Scientists think that Uranus may have been knocked onto its side when an Earth-sized object crashed into it while it was forming.

▲ Uranus has 13 rings. They reflect less light than Saturn's rings, so are not as easily seen.

I DON'T BELIEVE IT!

When Uranus was discovered in 1781, it was almost named *Georgium Sidus* (Georgian planet) after King George III of Great Britain. Uranus was instead chosen, after the ancient Greek god of the sky.

May, 1972:
The *Voyager* multiplanet mission was officially approved, and work began to build *Voyager 2* and its twin, *Voyager 1*.

20 August, 1977:
Voyager 2 was launched from Kennedy Space Flight Center, Florida, USA.

Ariel

Titania

▼ Uranus's five largest moons are Umbriel, Miranda, Oberon, Titania and Ariel.

Oberon

Umbriel

Miranda

Fact file: URANUS

Named after: The Greek god of the sky
Diameter: 51,118 kilometres (4.0 times Earth)
Distance from the Sun: 2873 million kilometres
Time to spin once: 17.2 hours
Time to orbit the Sun: 83.7 years
Average temperature: -195°C
Number of moons: 27

75 Uranus has 27 moons. Its biggest moon, Titania, is less than half the size of our Moon. Even though it is so small, it was spotted as long ago as 1787 by the astronomer William Herschel, who also discovered Uranus.

76 Only one spacecraft has visited Uranus – *Voyager 2*. It left Earth in 1977 and arrived at Uranus 11 years later in 1986. It is still the only spacecraft to have visited all four of the gas giants.

▼ *Voyager 2* discovered that Uranus has a tilted magnetic field. It also discovered ten of its moons and two of its rings.

24 January, 1986:
Voyager 2 made its closest approach to Uranus, coming within 81,500 kilometres of the mysterious planet's cloudtops.

24 January, 1986:
Images taken by *Voyager 2* revealed that Uranus's moon Miranda is actually covered in features such as craters, mountains, valleys and ridges.

25 August, 1989:
Voyager 2 reached Neptune, gathering important data about the eighth planet.

The farthest planet

77 The last of the Solar System's eight planets is Neptune. It is the smallest of the gas giants, but still nearly four times bigger than Earth. Like Uranus, it is an icy world made of hydrogen and helium, as well as water, ammonia and methane.

78 Neptune was the first planet found by mathematics. Astronomers noticed that Uranus was being tugged by the gravity of another large body, which affected its orbit. Calculations showed astronomers where to look, and in 1846, Neptune was found.

Dark storms in Neptune's atmosphere come and go every few years

Great Dark Spot

Fact file: NEPTUNE

Named after: The Roman god of the sea
Diameter: 49,528 kilometres (3.9 times Earth)
Distance from the Sun: 4495 million kilometres
Time to spin once: 16.1 hours
Time to orbit the Sun: 164 years
Average temperature: -200°C
Number of moons: 14

▶ Neptune's blue colour is caused by methane in its atmosphere.

▼ Clouds on Earth are made of water, but Neptune's clouds are made of chemicals including methane, ammonia and hydrogen sulphide.

79 Neptune's winds are the fastest in the Solar System. They race around Neptune at almost 2400 kilometres an hour. It is thought that heat bubbling up from Neptune's core creates these winds. Neptune's surface is also streaked with clouds, high in the atmosphere.

▲ Neptune's Great Dark Spot was a giant super-storm spinning anti-clockwise once every 16 days.

80 When *Voyager 2* photographed Neptune in 1989, it captured a large dark storm as big as Earth. The storm was called the Great Dark Spot. But when the Hubble Space Telescope was turned towards Neptune in 1994, the Great Dark Spot had disappeared.

81 Neptune has 14 moons, four of which are shepherd moons. The biggest, Triton, was discovered just 17 days after Neptune itself. Triton is so cold that it has ice volcanoes shooting out a mixture of liquid nitrogen, methane and dust.

▶ Triton's surface is covered with frozen nitrogen, a gas found on Earth.

I DON'T BELIEVE IT!

Neptune was discovered to be a planet in 1846, but it was first seen by the great astronomer, Galileo Galilei, 234 years earlier. Galileo thought he was looking at a star, not a planet.

Distant travellers

82 A comet is a mountain of rock and ice orbiting the Sun. Most comets are too far away for us to see, but occasionally they come closer to the Sun. The Sun's heat changes some of the ice into gas. Gas and dust flying off the comet form long, bright tails.

▼ The cloud or coma around a comet is made of dust and gas. Dust forms one of the comet's tails and gas forms a second tail.

Gas tail

Nucleus

Coma

Dust tail

83 A comet's tails always point away from the Sun. Sunlight and particles streaming away from the Sun – called the solar wind – sweep the tails back, away from the Sun.

▶ A comet's tails can be longer than the distance from the Earth to the Sun.

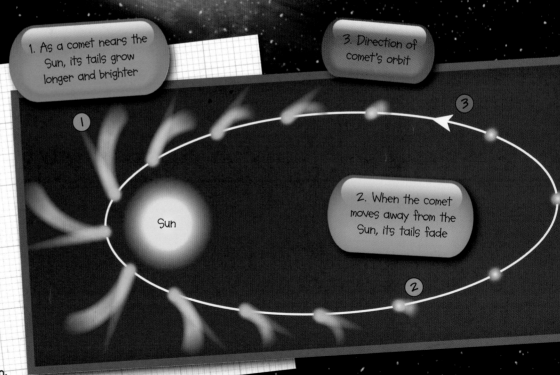

1. As a comet nears the Sun, its tails grow longer and brighter

3. Direction of comet's orbit

Sun

2. When the comet moves away from the Sun, its tails fade

84
In 1994, a comet slammed into the giant planet Jupiter. The comet was called Shoemaker-Levy 9. As it headed for Jupiter, it broke up. One after another, the pieces of the comet hurtled into Jupiter's atmosphere at more than 200 times the speed of a jet airliner, creating fireballs and huge dust clouds.

▶ Pieces of Shoemaker Levy 9 head for Jupiter like a string of pearls.

85
The whole Solar System may be surrounded by millions of comets! Scientists think that some of the comets we see come from a vast cloud of icy rocks that surrounds the entire Solar System. It's called the Oort Cloud. Others come from a closer region outside Neptune, called the Kuiper Belt.

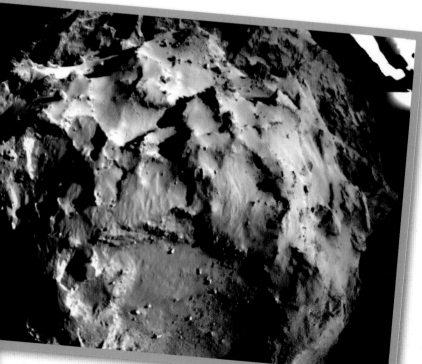

▲ Comet 67P appears in the sky every 6–7 years. On 12th November 2014, the European Space Agency's *Rosetta* spacecraft made history by landing a probe, *Philae*, on the comet. This image was taken by *Philae* during its descent.

86
The comets we see from time to time spend only a tiny part of their orbit near the Sun. The rest of the time, their long, thin orbit takes them far away to the outer reaches of the Solar System. These can take thousands of years to orbit the Sun. Some comets get caught up in much smaller orbits and appear every few years.

Dwarf planets

87 Dwarf planets are small worlds orbiting the Sun that are not big enough to be classed as planets. There are five 'official' dwarf planets, but dozens more have been found and may soon join the dwarf planet club.

NAME	DIAMETER (KILOMETRES)	DISCOVERED	NUMBER OF MOONS
PLUTO	2368	1930	5
ERIS	2326	2005	1
MAKEMAKE	1430	2005	0
HAUMEA	1240	2004	2
CERES	950	1801	0

▲ These are the first five dwarf planets to be officially recognized. More discoveries are certain to follow.

88 Pluto was a planet for 76 years. When Pluto was discovered in 1930, it became the Solar System's ninth planet. But when astronomers started finding more smaller worlds like Pluto, they decided to call them dwarf planets. So in 2006, Pluto became a dwarf planet. Pluto's orbit is oval-shaped, sometimes crossing inside Neptune's orbit.

▼ Ceres takes less than five years to orbit the Sun. Eris, much further away, takes 557 years.

Haumea

Eris

▶ Dwarf planet Pluto has five moons. The biggest is called Charon. A spacecraft called *New Horizons* will arrive at Pluto in 2015 to study the dwarf planet and its moons for the first time.

▶ Even though it is so far away, Makemake reflects just enough sunlight to be seen by large telescopes on Earth.

▶ Ceres may have a deep layer of ice under its thin, dusty crust.

89 Only one dwarf planet has been found in the Asteroid Belt between Mars and Jupiter. It's called Ceres, and it is also classed as the largest asteroid. The other dwarf planets orbit the Sun in the Kuiper Belt, beyond the farthest planets.

Makemake

Ceres

Pluto

90 Eris' discovery made astronomers rethink Pluto's status as a planet. Eris has more mass than Pluto, so both were classed as dwarf planets. Eris is the most distant dwarf planet, made of rock and ice.

▲ Eris has a tiny moon called Dysnomia. In Greek mythology, Dysnomia was the daughter of the Greek god Eris.

QUIZ

1. When was Pluto discovered?
2. Which dwarf planet is bigger than Pluto?
3. Which dwarf planet is further from the Sun — Haumea or Makemake?

Answers:
1. 1930 2. Eris 3. Makemake

▶ Haumea may have been set spinning very fast when something crashed into it millions of years ago.

91 Dwarf planet Haumea is a very strange shape. It spins so fast, once every four hours, that it has stretched out into the shape of an American football. Further out from Haumea, Makemake's surface has large amounts of solid frozen methane, found as a gas on Earth.

The search for life

92 Before the space age, some people thought intelligent creatures lived on Mars. So far, life has not been found on Mars or anywhere else in the Solar System, but scientists are still searching.

93 Two *Viking* spacecraft landed on Mars in 1976 to look for signs of life. When they tested the Martian soil, the results seemed to show signs of microscopic living organisms. However, scientists decided that the chemical activity found was not evidence of Martian life. In 2013, the *Curiosity* rover found evidence in Gale Crater of an environment that could have supported microscopic life billions of years ago.

▼ The *Curiosity* rover landed in Gale Crater on Mars on 6 August, 2012.

◄ When *Viking 2* landed on Mars in 1976, its cameras looked out on a rock-strewn part of the planet called Utopian Plain.

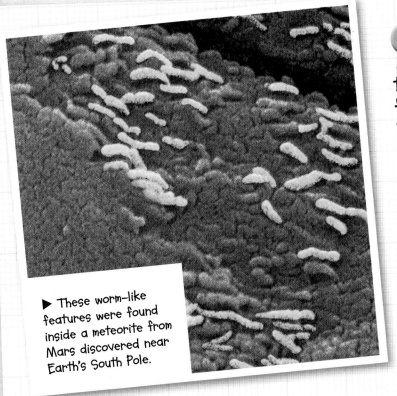

94 In 1996, scientists thought they may have finally found signs of Martian life. They discovered worm-like features in a meteorite from Mars that looked like microscopic fossils of bacteria. But other scientists disagreed. It will take more exploration to know for definite if life ever existed on Mars.

▶ These worm-like features were found inside a meteorite from Mars discovered near Earth's South Pole.

95 Life in the Solar System was previously thought to only be possible in a narrow band called the 'Goldilocks Zone'. But now scientists think life could exist elsewhere. One of the most promising possibilities is Jupiter's moon Europa, where there is thought to be an ocean of water underneath its icy surface.

FEAR. SACRIFICE. CONTACT.

E U R O P A   R E P O R T

▲ The 2013 feature film, *Europa Report*, tells the story of a fictional manned space mission to Jupiter's moon, Europa.

▼ The Goldilocks Zone was given its name because it's not too hot and not too cold – it's just right for life. It is also known as the habitable zone.

Mercury is far too hot for life to exist there

Venus is even hotter than Mercury

Earth is the right temperature for liquid water – essential for life

Mars is too cold and dry for complex life

The Solar System's Future

96 In the distant future, the Moon will look much smaller to our descendants. This is because its orbit is slowly increasing in size, moving it away from Earth. Every year the Moon moves about 3.8 centimetres further away from us.

▼ High tides on Earth are speeding up the Moon, causing it to move further away from Earth.

▶ The Moon is slowly spiralling away from Earth.

Key

① The Moon's gravity raises a bulge of water on Earth

② The spinning Earth drags the water ahead of the Moon

③ The water pulls on the Moon, speeding it up and increasing its orbit

Moon's orbit

Earth's rotation

97 The Sun is gradually growing bigger and brighter. This is because the amount of hydrogen gas in the Sun is decreasing over time. In about a billion years, it will begin to evaporate Earth's oceans.

98 In about four billion years, a galactic collision will take place. The Milky Way galaxy that includes our Solar System will collide with neighbouring Andromeda galaxy, although Earth and the Solar System should survive.

◄ When the Milky Way and Andromeda galaxies meet, they will merge together to form one enormous new galaxy.

99 About five billion years from now, the Sun will run out of hydrogen and other fuels it needs. Nuclear fusion will stop. The Sun will swell up into a massive red giant star and cool down.

► The red giant Sun will be over 200 times bigger than the Sun today — big enough to swallow the closest planets, perhaps including Earth.

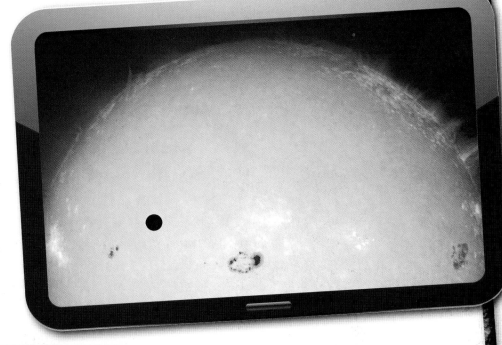

100 The red giant star will eventually blow away its outer layers of gas. This will leave a glowing halo of gas around the star. The remaining star will then shrink to become a tiny white dwarf. The white dwarf will cool and fade away over billions of years.

◄ The cloud of gas that will surround the shrinking Sun is called a planetary nebula.

Index

Page numbers in **bold** refer to main entries, those in *italics* refer to illustrations.